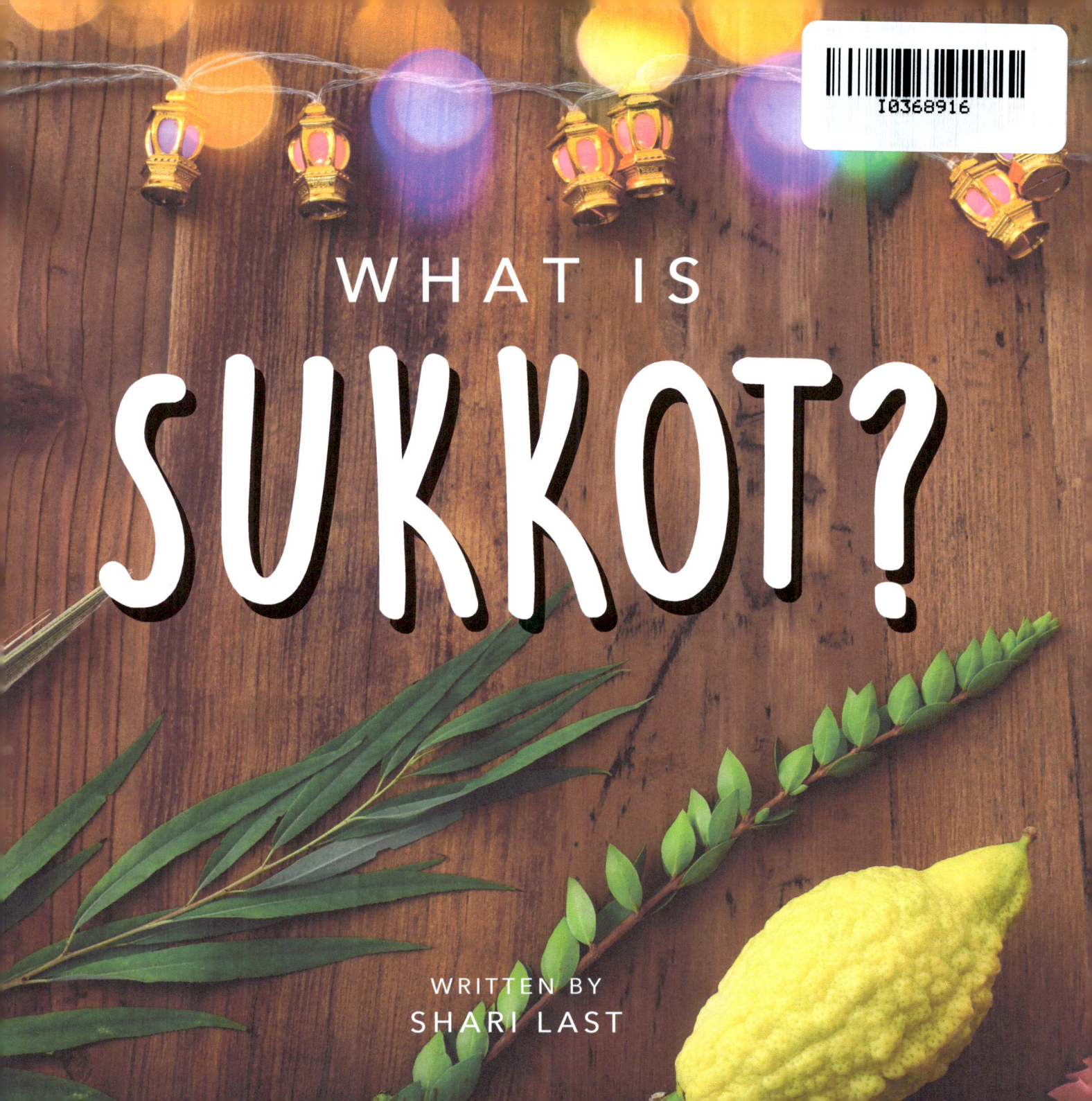

WHAT IS SUKKOT?

WRITTEN BY
SHARI LAST

THE FESTIVAL OF HUTS

One of the more unique Jewish holidays!

Sukkot celebrates how the Jews lived in huts while they journeyed through the desert, and relied on God for their safety.

You can probably imagine the ancient Jewish people, living in makeshift desert homes. What do you think happened when temperatures soared? Or during a sandstorm?

Well, on Sukkot, there's no need to imagine — Jewish people build their own huts in their backyards, or on their balconies, and spend seven days experiencing outdoor living. It's a bit like camping — a little cold, a little rough, but lots of fun with family and friends!

HARVEST HOLIDAY
Sukkot is one of the three Jewish harvest festivals. It marks the final harvest before winter begins.

ARE YOU READY TO FIND OUT MORE ABOUT SUKKOT?

WHEN IS SUKKOT?

Sukkot is a seven-day festival, with another two-day festival following on immediately afterwards. (In Israel, this additional festival lasts only one day).

Sukkot begins on the 15th of the Jewish month of Tishrei, just five days after Yom Kippur, the end of the High Holy Days.

WHY IS IT CALLED SUKKOT?

In Hebrew, *Sukkot* means "huts" or "booths", referring to the desert huts the Jews lived in. There are other names for this festival too: **The Day of the Gathering** (which refers to the harvest) and **The Time of Our Rejoicing** (which tells us this should be a happy festival).

Here is how Sukkot is written in Hebrew:

סוכות

THE HEBREW CALENDAR

The Hebrew calendar is lunar, so it is different to the "regular" calendar. Sukkot is the autumn harvest festival, so it usually falls in September or October.

CELEBRATING SUKKOT

Like most of the other Jewish festivals, Sukkot offers the opportunity to spend time with your family, pray with your community at synagogue, and enjoy festive meals. Unlike other festivals, Sukkot meals take place in huts, and the prayer services include waving a selection of branches and fruit in the air!

THE SUKKAH

Sukkot means "huts". The singular word is sukkah, a temporary dwelling built for the festival of Sukkot. During Sukkot, most Jewish people eat their meals in the sukkah.

THE FOUR SPECIES

The Four Species are an important symbolic part of Sukkot. They are used every day of Sukkot at the synagogue service or at home. We will learn more about the Four Species soon!

PRAYERS

Special prayers are recited every day of Sukkot. These include Hallel (poems of praise), the Prayer for Rain (since Sukkot marks the start of winter), and Hoshanot (a prayer based on an ancient ceremony).

THE WILLOW CEREMONY

Around 2,000 years ago, willow branches were placed against the altar of the Temple of Jerusalem. Worshippers walked around them, reciting prayers. Nowadays, at the daily Sukkot service, people walk around the synagogue, holding the Four Species, and reciting the Hoshanot prayer.

SUKKOT DAY BY DAY

SUKKOT FESTIVAL DAYS
DAYS 1–2

Sukkot is a seven-day holiday. The first two days are "festival" days, so they are similar to Shabbat — Jewish people cannot drive, write, work, go to school, spend money, or use electronic devices.

The days are spent going to synagogue, eating in the sukkah, and spending time with family and friends.

CHOL HAMOED
DAYS 3–6

The next five days are known as "chol hamoed". Driving, watching TV, etc. are allowed, but it's still Sukkot, so we continue to eat in the sukkah and shake the Four Species.

CHOL HAMOED / HOSHANAH RABBAH
DAY 7

The final day of chol hamoed is also called Hoshanah Rabbah. There is an extra-special Hoshanot service on this day. Apart from that, it is like the rest of chol hamoed.

SHEMINI ATZERET FESTIVAL DAYS
DAYS 8-9

Immediately after Sukkot there is another, related festival. It is called Shemini Atzeret, which means the Eighth Day of Assembly. It is another "festival" day, so work is not allowed.

In Israel, Shemini Atzeret lasts one day, while outside of Israel, it lasts two days. The second day is known as Simchat Torah, and is one of the highlights of the year for kids. Find out why in a few pages!

WHAT IS A SUKKAH?

The most important part of Sukkot is the sukkah. It reminds the Jewish people of the time their ancestors lived in temporary huts in the desert. It symbolises how fragile life is and how much we rely on God. There are very specific rules about what counts as a sukkah – you can't just use a garden shed!

The roof must be open enough to the sky that you can see the stars through it.

The roof must be made of plant material, but it can't still be growing in the ground. Therefore, you can't build a sukkah under a tree.

A sukkah must have at least two and a half walls. They can be made of anything.

A special blessing is said before eating in the sukkah.

The Torah's instructions are to live in the sukkah, but most people choose to eat their meals in the sukkah. Some do try to sleep in it as well – but this is much more dependent on the weather!

THE ROOF

The roof material is called *s'chach*. Many people use laurel branches as *s'chach*. It's also common to use a special mat of bamboo. It's made especially for Sukkot, so the sticks are open enough to see the stars through them.

A man places a bamboo mat on his sukkah.

DECORATIONS

It is customary to decorate the sukkah and make it really festive! Children often create posters and decorations at school. Some people hang fairy lights. Because it's also a harvest festival, many people decorate the sukkah with fruits and vegetables.

LOOK AT MY SUKKAH!

As long as it fulfils the technical laws, there are no limits as to what your sukkah can look like!

SUKKAH SETS

It is fun to build a sukkah from scratch, but it an be tricky. You can buy easy-to-assemble sukkahs that fit together easily, with plastic or metal poles and canvas walls that are lightweight, and waterproof.

Decorating my sukkah is my favourite thing about Sukkot!

We use different sheets for our sukkah walls every year, so it never looks the same!

DID YOU KNOW?

You don't have to eat in the sukkah if it rains. Some families build a removable roof on top of the *s'chach*. This protects the sukkah from rain, but can be removed when it's time to use the sukkah.

I can't wait to eat in the sukkah with all my cousins!

We live in a warm country so our sukkah is open on one side.

Almost every family in my apartment block builds their own sukkah!

I decorate my sukkah with lots of greenery.

THE FOUR SPECIES

There is a special commandment just for Sukkot, called the Four Species. On each day of Sukkot, a blessing is said over four kinds of plant, which are then waved in six directions: up, down, forward, backward, right, and left. This is an important symbolic part of Sukkot — but it probably seems very strange!

Lulav – palm branch

The Four Species

Hadassim – three myrtle branches

Etrog – citron fruit

Aravot – two willow branches

In Hebrew, the Four Species are called the Arba Minim.

SYMBOLIC MEANING

Some say that the shape of each of the Four Species represents a part of the human body:

Lulav – spine
Hadassim leaves – eyes
Aravot leaves – mouth
Etrog – heart

Combining them shows that we want to serve God with our whole body.

UNITED WE STAND

Another explanation is that the Four Species represent the four different kinds of Jewish people. By holding them together, it shows we want the Jewish people to be united.

ALL AROUND US

And why are the Four Species waved in six directions? Because God is here, there, and everywhere.

The Four Species are waved every day of Sukkot, apart from Shabbat.

You might not think it would be important, but there is some debate among rabbis about the order in which the Four Species are waved. My family tradition is to wave them up, forward, right, backward, left, and down.

THE PITOM

Only whole Etrogs are kosher (permitted to use according to Jewish law). There is a small, brown piece at the tip of most Etrogs. It is called the Pitom, and if it breaks off, the Etrog cannot be used. Some types of Etrog grow without a Pitom. Those are fine.

The Pitom is not the stalk that was attached to the tree – it's on the other end.

DID YOU KNOW?

Jewish people are meant to choose the most beautiful Four Species they can, so they take their Etrog shopping very seriously.

ETROG BOX

Many people use an Etrog box to store their Etrog and ensure the Pitom doesn't break off. Some Etrog boxes are made of silver and are bought as a wedding present. Many are passed down as family heirlooms.

PREPARATION

The laws are very particular about how to set up the Four Species before you use them. The Lulav should be in the centre, with the myrtle branches on the right, and the willow branches on the left.

READY TO GO!

Hold the Etrog in the left hand with the Pitom pointing down. Hold the Lulav and branches in your right hand. Place your hands together, say the blessing, turn the Etrog so the Pitom points up, and then wave in all six directions.

USHPIZIN

A big part of Judaism is welcoming guests and being generous to others. On each night of Sukkot, as people sit down to their meal in the sukkah, there's a tradition to welcome a "guest" from the Torah. The "guests" are seven great figures from Jewish history and they are welcomed with a special prayer.

1. ABRAHAM
The founder of Judaism.

2. ISAAC
Abraham's son and one of the three fathers of Judaism.

3. JACOB
Isaac's son and the third father of Judaism.

4. JOSEPH
יוסף

Jacob's son – one of the twelves tribes of Israel.

5. MOSES
משה

The prophet and leader who brought the Jewish people out of Egypt.

6. AARON
אהרון

Moses's brother and the first High Priest of the Jewish people.

7. DAVID
דוד

A prophet and one of the most famous kings of Israel.

DID YOU KNOW?

Ushpizin is Aramaic for "guests". The prayer is in Aramaic, an ancient language. The Hebrew alphabet is based on the Aramaic alphabet.

HOSHANAH RABBAH

The seventh day of Sukkot is a special day called Hoshanah Rabbah. It is the day God's decree for the year ahead will be finalised. On Rosh Hashanah (the Jewish New Year) the decree was written, on Yom Kippur (the Day of Atonement), it was sealed. On Hoshanah Rabbah, it is completely finalised.

SPECIAL HOSHANOT PRAYER

A special Hoshanot prayer service takes place. Instead of walking around the synagogue once, we walk around seven times. Then a bundle of five willow branches is hit against the ground. This symbolises the hope that our sins should fall away.

SHEMINI ATZERET

A new festival begins the day after Sukkot. Shemini Atzeret is related to Sukkot, but not technically part of it, though I always think it feels like part of the same holiday. Shemini Atzeret is a festival day, so people go to synagogue and enjoy family meals. There are different opinions about whether people should still eat in the sukkah. Some do, and some don't, but no one says the blessing. Additionally, the Four Species are not waved on Shemini Atzeret.

SIMCHAT TORAH

Outside of Israel, Shemini Atzeret continues over to a second day. This day is known as Simchat Torah, which means Celebration of the Torah. On this day, we finish reading the Torah in the prayer service. Every week of the year, on Shabbat, a portion of the Torah is read. We finally get to the end of the the whole Torah on Simchat Torah. To celebrate, everyone sings and dances around the synagogue, carrying the Torah srolls.

Best of all, adults hand out candy to the kids. My friends and I have a competition to see who can collect the most!

TRADITIONAL FOODS
EATEN ON SUKKOT

STUFFED CABBAGE

Stuffed foods are symbolic of being full of blessings. They also reflect the harvest season, when produce is plentiful. Stuffed cabbage is a particular Sukkot favourite. Cabbage leaves are stuffed with rice and beef and stewed in a tomato or sweet-and-sour sauce. Some people stuff peppers as well.

KREPLACH

Another stuffed food, kreplach are eastern European boiled dumplings, stuffed with ground beef. They are usually served in chicken soup, and are always appreciated on a cold night in the sukkah!

FALL PRODUCE

Dishes made with fall foods, such as pumpkin and squash, are popular on this harvest festival. If you can think of a way to stuff them — even better!

CHALLAH IN HONEY

Fifteen days before Sukkot was Rosh Hashanah, the Jewish New Year. To ask God for a sweet year, apples and challah are dipped in honey. Sukkot ends off the new-year festive period, so we continue to dip challah in honey as we are still praying for a sweet year.

AROUND THE WORLD

There are many Jewish communities across the globe, each with their own culture and history. Let's discover traditions from around the world!

SYRIAN JEWS
Syrian sukkahs are traditionally decorated with the "Seven Species". These are the seven types of crops that are mentioned in the Torah: wheat, barley, grapes, figs, pomegranates, olives, and dates.

SEPHARDI JEWS
Some Sephardi Jews go the extra mile when welcoming Ushpizin guests to their sukkah. They set up a special chair for them in the sukkah, and leave a pile of holy books on it.

GERMANY
It is traditional to end meals with *lebkuchen*, honey cookies topped with nuts.

USA
It's so hot on Sukkot in Florida, that some families bring air conditioning units into their sukkah. In New York, however, it can be cold enough to need scarves and gloves in the sukkah!

BUKHARIAN JEWS

Bukharian Jews, originally from Uzbekistan, decorate their sukkahs with colourful silks and fabrics. Often, the floor is laid with rugs and pillows to sit on, and fruit and fragrant herbs are hung from the s'chach.

GREAT BRITAIN

On the first two days of Sukkot, many British children will go on a "Sukkah crawl". They visit their neighbours and give their sukkahs a score out of ten. Families often leave candy or other treats in the sukkah in hopes of receiving a higher grade!

VENICE

Some Venetian Jews have an old custom to set the table in the sukkah with pomegranates and corn in celebration of the harvest. They call their Sukkot tables *tavola dell' angelo* (table of the angels).

WORLDWIDE

A recent custom is to welcome seven female Ushpizin at the Sukkot meals, in addition to the seven men. The female "guests" are: Sarah, Rachel, Rebecca, Leah, Miriam, Abigail, and Esther.

SUKKOT GREETINGS

If you have any Jewish friends and you want to wish them a happy Sukkot, here are a few ways to say it:

"HAPPY SUKKOT!"

"CHAG SUKKOT SAMEACH!"
Pronunciation: *Khuh-g Sook-ot Sum-ay-ukh*
Hebrew meaning: "Happy Sukkot!"

"CHAG SAMEACH!"
Pronunciation: *Khuh-g Sum-ay-ukh*
Hebrew meaning: "Happy festival!"

"MO'ADIM LESIMCHAH!"
Pronunciation: *Mo-uh-dim Leh-sim-khuh*
Hebrew meaning: "May your times be happy!"
Used mostly on the days of chol hamoed.

"AH GEZUNTE VINTER!"
Pronunciation: *Uh Gez-int-uh Vin-tuh*
Yiddish meaning: "Happy winter!"
Said after Sukkot has ended.

NOTE
The "kh" sound in "Chag", "Sameach", and "Chatimah" is a guttural sound you make at the back of your throat. Or you can just use an "h" sound.

LET'S MAKE STUFFED CABBAGE!

Warming and tasty, stuffed cabbage is the ultimate Sukkot dish. It's fun to make too! This recipe serves 3-4 people, but double it if you need to!

For the cabbage
- 8 cabbage leaves
- 500g ground beef
- 1 onion
- 1/2 cup rice, cooked
- 1 egg
- 2 tbsp tomato sauce
- salt
- pepper
- garlic powder
- cumin

For the sauce
- 2 cups tomato sauce
- 3 tbsp lemon juice
- 3 tbsp sugar
- salt
- pepper

Stuffed cabbage is also known as *Holishkes* or *Holopshes*.

MEATLESS ALTERNATIVES

You can replace the ground beef with meat-free mince, or you can use rice only as the stuffing. Just be sure to add a bit of extra seasoning.

Method

1. Boil the cabbage leaves in water for a few minutes to soften them.
2. In a bowl, mix the rest of the cabbage ingredients to create the stuffing.
3. Divide the stuffing between the cabbage leaves. Roll it into circles or cylinder shapes and wrap carefully with the leaves, overlapping the edges so it doesn't spill out. (You can secure the rolled-up leaves with toothpicks if you want to make sure!)
4. Place the stuffed cabbages into an oven-proof dish.
5. In a separate bowl, mix the sauce ingredients together, then pour over the cabbages.
6. Cover the dish tightly and cook on 160°C for 90 minutes.

SUKKOT CRAFT IDEAS

Sukkah Posters

Let all your creativity come out! Design some posters to hang in your sukkah. Think about what picture you want to draw. Decide if you will use markers, pencils, or paint. Then go for it! If your sukkah doesn't have a roof, perhaps seal your poster inside sticky plastic or a see-through folder to protect it from rain.

Paper Chains

It's fun to make colourful paper chains to hang across your sukkah. Take coloured paper — or use pages from a magazine. Cut the paper into strips. Make one strip into a hoop and stick, tape, or staple the ends together. (Ask an adult to help with the stapler!) Then thread the next strip through, and the next, until you are done. How long will your paper chain be?

AUTUMN CRAFTS

Celebrate the harvest season by finding autumnal objects to decorate the sukkah. Big, beautiful leaves make gorgeous wall-hangings, and pine cones can be painted or strung together to create amazing works of art!

HANGING DECORATIONS

Sukkah decorations can be anything. Gather your friends and create some hanging decorations using string and beads. If you don't have beads, think about what else you could use. Fruits and vegetables? Recycled materials? Shells and stones? You can paint old objects and turn them into something new!

Tell Me More!
NEW IDEAS FOR KIDS

First published in Great Britain in 2024
by TELL ME MORE Books

Text copyright ©2024 Shari Last
Design copyright ©2024 Shari Last

ISBN: 978-1-917200-04-2

Picture credits: Thanks to Adobe Stock; Thirteen-J at Unsplash; Zachi Evenor, Beth H, Michael Radwin, and Zeevveez at Flickr; and Yossi Broyer, Chameleon's Eye, denisgo, Maksim Dubinsky, David Cohen, Hadasit, Kavram, Shlomit Koslowe, Inna Reznik, Pixel-Shot, Avishag Shuva, and Tomertu at Shutterstock.com.

All rights reserved. Without limiting the rights under the copyright reserved above, no part of this publication may be reproduced, stored in, or introduced into a retrieval system, or transmitted, in any form, or by any means (electronic, mechanical, photocopying, recording or otherwise), without the prior written permission of the copyright owner.

WWW.TELLMEMOREBOOKS.COM

THINGS I'VE LEARNED...

Visit our website if you want to learn more about all sorts of interesting things!

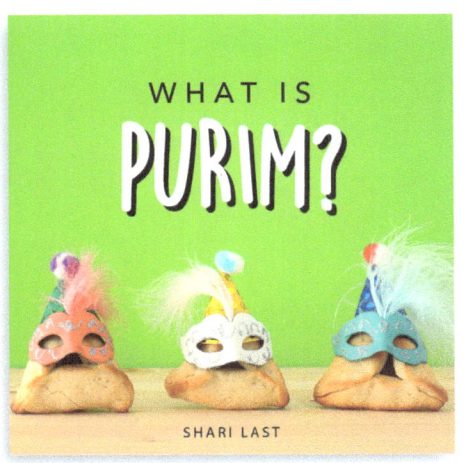
What is Purim?

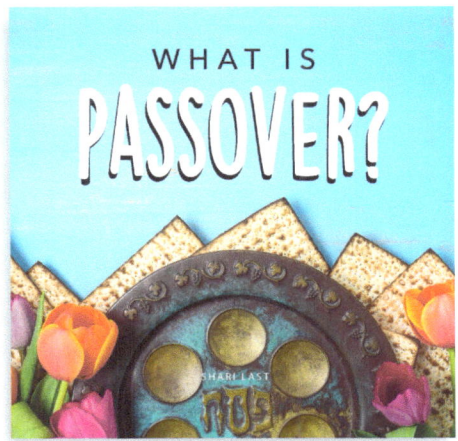
What is Passover?

What is Hanukkah?

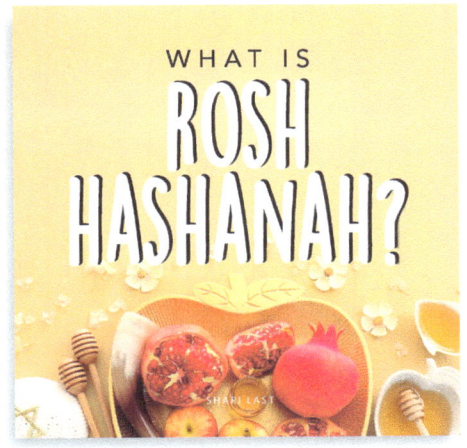
What is Rosh Hashanah?

What is Shavuot?

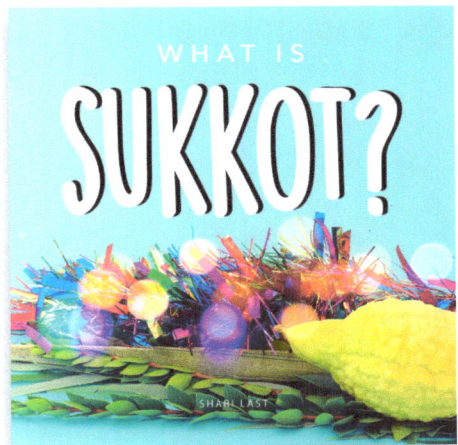
What is Sukkot?

COLLECT THEM ALL!

WWW.TELLMEMOREBOOKS.COM

www.ingramcontent.com/pod-product-compliance
Lightning Source LLC
Chambersburg PA
CBHW050749110526
44591CB00002B/19